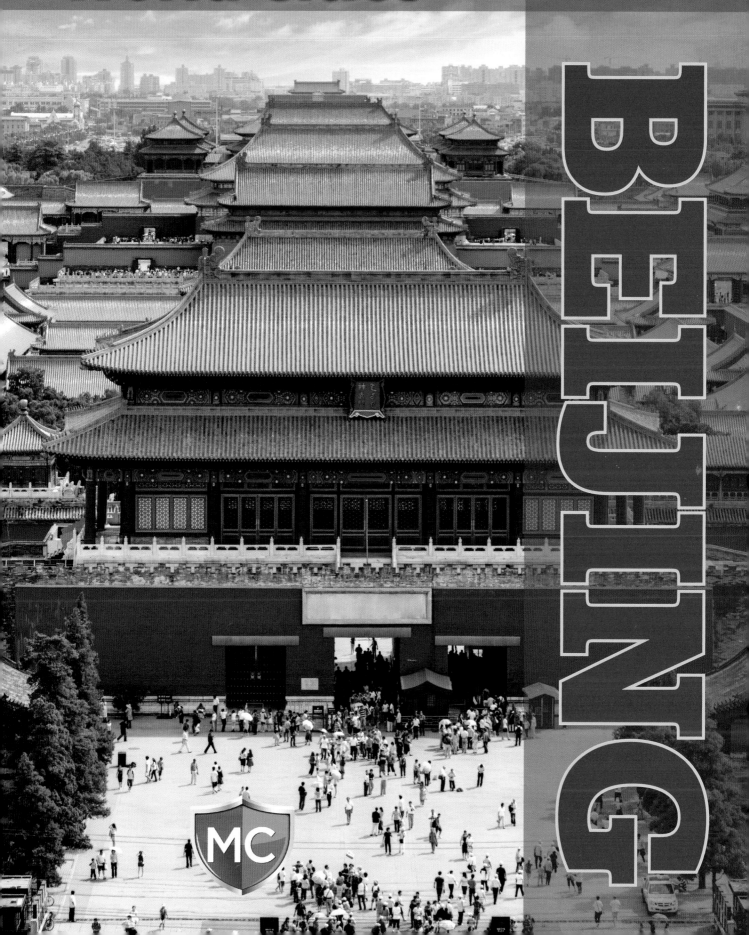

MAJOR
World Cities

BEIJING

MC

Mason Crest
450 Parkway Drive, Suite D
Broomall, PA 19008
www.masoncrest.com
Developed and produced by Mason Crest

Printed and bound in the United States of America.

First printing
9 8 7 6 5 4 3 2 1

Series ISBN: 978-1-4222-3538-6
ISBN: 978-1-4222-3539-3
ebook ISBN: 978-1-4222-8359-2

Library of Congress Cataloging-in-Publication Data is on file with the publisher.

Additional images

Cover: Anastasia Sushko/Dreamstime.
AA Photolibrary: 36, 37t; AFP: /Stephen Shaver 42; AKG London: /Erich Lessing 37b; Associated Press Picture Library: 41br; CORBIS: /Hulton Getty Collection 41tl, /Library of Congress 101; E.T. Archive: 8r, 9b, 11t, /Berry Hill Galleries, N.Y. 26t, /Bibliotheque Nationale, Paris 41tr, /British Museum 19b, 22b, /Musec Guimet 40, /National Palace Museum, Taiwan 81, /Royal Danish Naval Museum 9t; Eye Ubiquitous: /James Davis Travel Photography 22t, 23t; Sally & Richard Greenhill: Cover BR, 5cr, 18t, 20t, 20b, 25b, 26b, 27b, 27b, /S.A.C.U. 13t, 27t, /Sam Greenhill 5bl, 32t; Robert Harding Picture Library: 14t, 14b, 15b, 15t, 16t, 16b, 17t, 21t, 25t, 28b, 29b, 33t, 34, 35t, 38t; Rex Features: Cover TR, 10b, 11b, 18b, 32b, 43t; Frank Spooner Pictures: 24b, 33b, 38-39b; TRIP: /K. Cardwell 31b, M. Good 4, 17b, /T. Bognar 23b, /Terry Wright 35b. Dreamstime.com: Sang Lei 12t; Fotokon 12b; Shannon Fagan 13b; Robert Paul Van Beets 19t; Shaowen1994 21b; Linqong 24t; Xi Zhang 28t; Dk88888 29t; Grigor Atanasov 30; Zjm7100 31t; Zhaojiankang 39t; Calvin86 43

Words in **bold** are explained in the glossary on pages 46 and 47.

MAJOR
World Cities

BEIJING

BERLIN

LONDON

MOSCOW

NEW YORK

PARIS

ROME

SYDNEY

CONTENTS

INTRODUCTION

The city of Beijing is the capital of the People's **Republic** of China and stands in the northeast of the country. Its urban area covers just over 528 square miles

(about 1,300 square kilometers), but the **municipality** is about 6,336 square miles (16,800 square kilometers) and contains more than 21 million people. Beijing is the country's political and cultural heart, even though it is only the second largest city. The largest is Shanghai, further south, with a population of more than 15 million.

City layout

The center of modern Beijing is known as the Old City. It is **symmetrical**, and divided into two parts, called the Inner City and the Outer City. Both were once enclosed in high walls. The Inner City was built in the 15th century. This area contains the Forbidden City, a collection of palaces where China's emperors lived, and the **Imperial** City, where nobles lived. The 16th-century Outer City, to the south, was built for ordinary people.

▲ Beijing is a striking mix of old and new. In this view of the capital, the palaces of the 15th-century Forbidden City stand in front of towering modern skyscrapers.

FAST FACTS
BEIJING

STATUS
Capital of the People's Republic of China;
one of China's four independent municipalities

AREA (municipality)
6,336 square miles (16,800 square km)

POPULATION
21,150,000 (2013)

GOVERNING BODY
People's Congress of Beijing Municipality;
Beijing People's Government

CLIMATE
Temperatures average 14 to 34°F (-10 to 1°C)
in January and 70 to 88°F (21 to 31°C) in July

TIME ZONE
Greenwich Mean Time plus 8 hours

CURRENCY
Renminbi (People's Money)
1 yuan = 10 jiao = 100 fen

OFFICIAL LANGUAGE
Putonghua (Mandarin Chinese)

Building boom

A **Communist** government came to power in China in 1949 (see page 11). Under its rule, Beijing rapidly expanded beyond the Inner and Outer Cities. Builders knocked down the old city walls and other ancient structures. They created large numbers of new buildings, including high-rise tower blocks and factories. Building and demolition work still goes on all day and night.

Local government

Beijing is an independent municipality, one of four in China. Its central area is divided into ten districts and the countryside around is divided into eight counties. Beijing is run by a group called a Congress, chosen by the Chinese Communist Party. Congress members elect the city government.

The Zhongnanhai compound is guarded by ▲
soldiers of the People's Liberation Army.

Heavy downpours ➤
of warm rain are
common during
Beijing summers,
but the city's
many cyclists are
well prepared.

National government

China's national government is based in Beijing. Its members belong to the Chinese Communist Party. The government meets in the Great Hall of the People in Tiananmen Square (see page 14). Top government members live in the Zhongnanhai compound. This is known as the New Forbidden City because the public are not allowed inside.

MAPS OF THE CITY

These maps show you Beijing as it is today. The street map shows you where many of the buildings, parks, and other places mentioned in this book are located. The inset map gives a closer view of the halls and palaces of the Forbidden City, at the very center of the Chinese capital.

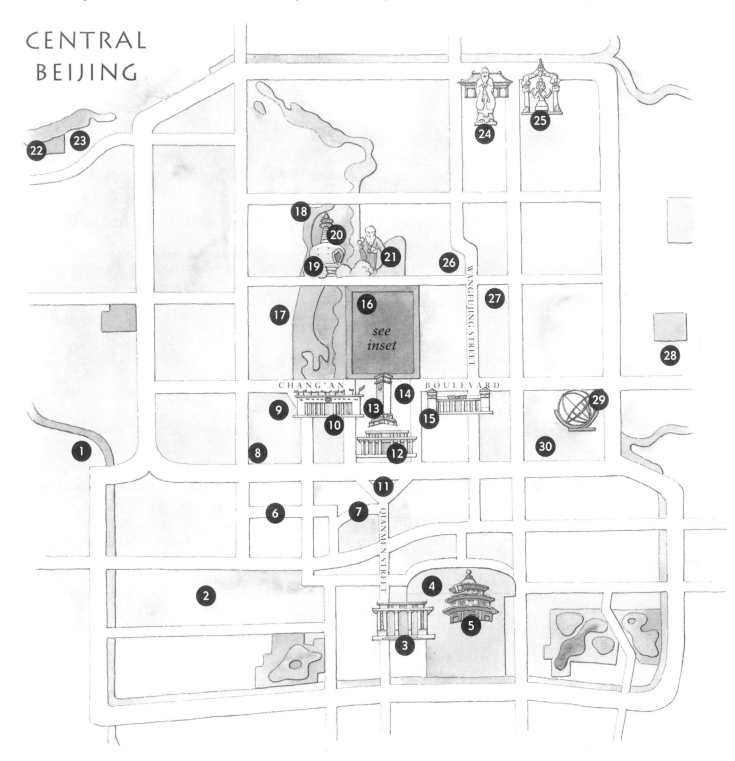

CENTRAL BEIJING

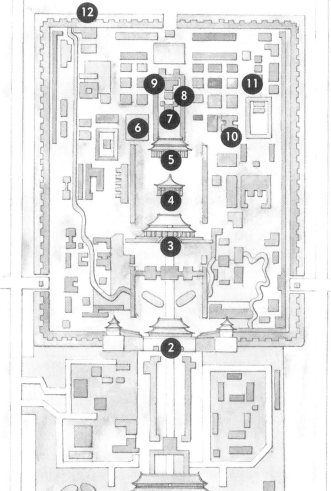

1 Temple of the White Cloud

2 Niujie Mosque

3 Natural History Museum

4 Tiantan (Temple of Heaven) Park

5 Hall of Prayer for Good Harvests

6 Liulichang Street

7 Dazhalan Hutong

8 South Cathedral

9 Beijing Concert Hall

10 Great Hall of the People

11 Qianmen (Front Gate)

12 Mao Zedong Mausoleum

13 Monument to the People's Heroes

14 Tiananmen Square

15 Museum of Chinese History and Revolution

16 The Forbidden City

17 Zhongnanhai area

18 Beihai (North Lake) Park

19 Jade Island

20 White Dagoba

21 Jingshan Park

22 Beijing Zoo

23 Beijing Exhibition Center Theatre

24 Confucius Temple

25 Lama Temple

26 China Art Gallery

27 Dongsi Mosque

28 Jianguomenwai area

29 Ancient Observatory

30 Main Railway Station

1 Tiananmen (Gate of Heavenly Peace)

2 Wumen (Meridian Gate)

3 Hall of Supreme Harmony

4 Hall of Middle Harmony

5 Hall of Preserving Harmony

6 Hall of Mental Cultivation

7 Palace of Heavenly Purity

8 Hall of Union

9 Palace of Earthly Tranquility

10 Hall of Clocks

11 Hall of Jewellery

12 Palace Moat

BEIJING'S EARLY HISTORY

 The area of China where Beijing now stands became important because it was a meeting place for traders. The first city grew up there about 2,500 years ago. It was destroyed in the 3rd century BCE, and a new city was built. For centuries afterwards the Chinese fought northern **nomads** for control of the area, and the city changed hands, and names, several times.

Invaders from the north

In the 10th century BCE, northern China was invaded by the **Khitan**. They took over the city, made it their second capital, and called it Yanjing. In the 12th century the Khitan were defeated by another tribe from the north, the **Jurchen**. They made the city their capital and renamed it Zhongdu. In 1215 Zhongdu was burned to the ground by the **Mongols**, led by the mighty **Genghis Khan**.

◄ Khubilai Khan was Emperor of China from 1279 until 1294. He died in 1295 and his body was taken back to Mongolia. No one knows where he was buried.

Mongol rule

In 1266 Khubilai Khan, grandson of Genghis, began to build a new city just north of where Zhongdu had stood. It became the capital of the Mongol Empire. The city had two names—Dadu, Chinese for "Great Capital"; and Khanbalik, Mongolian for "City of the Khan." Its Imperial Palace and other grand buildings made it a splendid sight. The Italian traveller Marco Polo carried reports of its magnificence back to Europe. Khubilai Khan also founded the Yuan **dynasty**, which ruled China from 1279 to 1368.

▲ This painting on silk shows the Forbidden City's magnificent palaces and courtyards. They were built by 200,000 workers.

In the 18th century, ➤ demand grew in the West for Chinese goods such as tea. China limited trade and made all foreign merchants live in the port of Guangzhou (Canton). This painting shows the Danish, British, and Dutch embassies there.

The Ming dynasty

In August 1368 Chinese rebels drove the Mongols from Dadu. The rebels then set up the Ming dynasty and moved the capital city south to Nanjing. The Ming emperor Yongle came to power in 1403. He wanted to move back to northern China, to keep a watchful eye on the Mongols over the border. So in 1406 construction work began on a new city just south of Dadu. The Forbidden City and many other structures that make up Beijing's Old City were then built. In 1421 Yongle moved in, and the city became known as Beijing, meaning "Northern Capital."

The Qing dynasty

In 1644 the **Manchus** invaded China, drove out the Ming, and set up the Qing dynasty. The Qing emperors constructed many new buildings in Beijing, in places such as the Summer Palace (see page 17). They treated Chinese people badly, and only Manchus were allowed to live in the Inner City.

War and rebellion

At first Qing rule brought peace and wealth to China. But by the 19th century, the dynasty was corrupt and weak. The Chinese were defeated by Europeans in the **Opium Wars**, while the Qing rulers were almost toppled by the **Taiping Rebellion**. In 1895 Japan defeated China in war. Meanwhile, countries such as Britain began to take over Chinese land and industry. But **Dowager Empress** Cixi did not allow any reforms to be made.

The Taiping Rebellion lasted from 1850 to 1864. The British ▲ and French helped the imperial army defeat the rebels.

20TH-CENTURY BEIJING

In 1900 a group of Chinese peasants known as the **Boxers** decided to end foreign interference in China. They went to Beijing, surrounded its embassies and killed many people. The siege lasted 55 days, ending only when a force of 20,000 foreign troops came to the rescue. The Qing then had to pay a huge fine and give more rights to foreigners.

From empire to republic

Despite reforms, the Qing remained weak. In 1908 they grew weaker when Cixi died and was replaced by Puyi, a three-year-old boy. Meanwhile, reformers led by Dr Sun Yat-sen were plotting to end the empire. Sun's chance came in 1911 when revolts broke out. He took over and, in 1912, set up a **republican** government in Beijing, with himself as president.

▲ These Boxers were captured by American cavalry troops during the rebellion. The troops are just visible in the background.

▲ The reign of the child-emperor Puyi came to an end in 1911, but he lived in the Forbidden City until 1924.

Republican failures

Sun Yat-sen was unable to restore order in China, so he gave up the presidency. Rival warlords began to fight in the north, and Beijing fell into decay. Republican rule also failed to end foreign influence. After the **First World War** (1914–18), areas of German land in China were given to Japan. This led to protests in Beijing on May 4, 1919. Communist ideas began to spread, and then, in 1921, the Chinese Communist Party was founded.

在毛澤東的勝利旗幟下前進

▲ In this 1949 poster, Mao Zedong stands in front of the five-starred flag of the People's Republic of China and the hammer-and-sickle flag that represents Communism.

The People's Republic

In 1937 the Japanese army attacked Beijing and took over the city until the end of the **Second World War**. The Kuomintang returned to power after the war, but fighting began between Nationalists and Communists. The Communists won. On October 1, 1949, their leader, Mao Zedong, proclaimed the foundation of the People's Republic of China in Tiananmen Square.

Communist government

Under Communist rule, Beijing became China's capital again. Tiananmen Square was rebuilt and has been the site of many events, including ceremonies to mark the death of Mao in 1976. In 1989 a pro-**democracy** demonstration took place there, when the army killed many protesters. Communist rule continues under new President Jiang Zemin. But Beijing is changing fast.

The 1989 demonstrations in Tiananmen Square ▲ were led by students. After six weeks, people watching television all over the world saw the People's Liberation Army crush the peaceful protests.

Civil war

In 1923 Sun Yat-sen and his **Kuomintang** (Nationalist Party) set up a government in the southern port of Guangzhou. When Sun died in 1925, Chiang Kai-shek took over. He led Nationalist and Communist troops north, hoping to defeat the warlords and unify the country. Instead, **civil war** broke out between the Nationalists and Communists. In 1928 Chiang seized power from the warlords in Beijing. He set up a government in Nanjing, to the south, which became China's capital.

THE PEOPLE OF BEIJING

In 1949, when the **Communists** took power in China, only about one million people lived in Beijing. Since then, millions more have poured into the city to work in its new government offices and industries. In the early Communist years, the population grew because Mao Zedong encouraged people to have many children to make China strong. Now the government is trying to stop Beijing's population of about 21 million from growing any larger.

After nearly four decades, ▲ China's one-child policy was relaxed in 2016.

Population control

The government decided to stop population growth in Beijing, and in China as a whole, because it feared that farmers would not be able to grow enough food for all the people. So in the late 1970s, the government ruled that people could have only one child. It was not until 2016, with much of the population growing older and leaving the work force, that the government changed its policy to two children per family.

Old and young

There is a growing difference between the lifestyles of the old and young in Beijing. Many people who grew up in the Mao years cling to strict Communist ways. They work hard and do not spend money on luxuries. Most walk or cycle around Beijing, and dress in plain, dark clothes. Young people are making the most of Beijing's growing wealth. Many buy fashionable clothes and drive cars.

◄ These women are doing their morning dance exercises in the Temple of Heaven park.

Population mix

About 96 percent of people living in Beijing are **ethnic Chinese,** known as Han-Chinese. Members of China's 55 minority groups also live in the city.

The Hui (Chinese people who converted to Islam in the 10th century AD) are one of the largest minority groups in Beijing. More than 400,000 of them live in the city. Their main place of worship is the Niujie Mosque (see page 23). There are two other large minority groups in Beijing: the Manchus and the **Mongols.**

▼ People from East and West now more commonly meet and conduct business in Beijing than ever before.

People have lived in the Beijing region for thousands of years. In 1929 a skull was found near Zhoukoudian, about 34 miles (55 km) from central Beijing. It belonged to a member of an early human species and was about half a million years old. The species is now known as Beijing Man. The model above shows what a member of the species probably looked like.

Newcomers

In the Mao years, people from the countryside were not allowed to move to cities. Now many *waidiren* (people from outside towns) come to Beijing looking for work. China also opened up to foreigners after Mao's death, so Beijing contains a growing number of foreign business people. The government did not like the Chinese to come into contact with foreigners and their democratic ideas, and the two groups still live in separate areas.

ARCHITECTURE

Beijing's Forbidden City is one of the architectural masterpieces of the world. Many other amazing structures are scattered among the busy streets of the capital, as well as in the surrounding countryside.

This entrance is part of the Palace ▲ of Heavenly Purity, which contained the bedroom of the Ming emperors.

The Forbidden City

The Forbidden City, once the private domain of the emperors, was built from 1406 to 1421. Its 800 buildings cover about 250 acres (101 hectares) and are enclosed by a moat and a high wall. The Outer Court contains the Halls of Supreme Harmony, Middle Harmony, and Preserving Harmony, where the emperors carried out public duties. The Inner Court contains the Palace of Heavenly Purity, where the emperors lived, the Palace of Earthly Tranquility, and the Hall of Union.

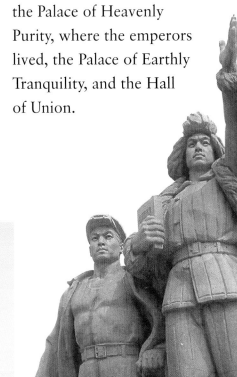

Tiananmen Square

Tiananmen (The Gate of Heavenly Peace) is south of the Forbidden City and leads into Tiananmen Square, the largest square in the world. Standing here is the Monument to the People's Heroes, dedicated to the soldiers who died fighting for the Communist revolution. Also here are The Great Hall of the People and the Mao Zedong Mausoleum.

▲ The Hall of Prayer for Good Harvests was struck by lightning in 1889 and burned to the ground. It was rebuilt a year later.

The Temple of Heaven

The Temple of Heaven (Tiantan) is a group of buildings in the Outer City's Tiantan Park. The group includes the stunning Hall of Prayer for Good Harvests, completed in 1420. The emperors went to the hall on the shortest day of every year. There they offered prayers and sacrifices to Heaven in the hope that this would bring good crops and good fortune. The hall is round because the ancient Chinese thought that Heaven was round.

The Great Wall

The Great Wall of China was originally many separate walls built to keep northern **nomads** out of the country. The walls were linked in the 3rd century BC, and the Ming emperors (see page 9) rebuilt most of the structure. In the 1980s the Communists began to restore the wall again. Two restored sections in the Beijing area now attract many visitors: the Badaling Great Wall, about 45 miles (72 km) from the capital; and the Mutianyu Great Wall, about 50 miles (80 km) away.

THE UNDERGROUND CITY

In the 1960s the two Communist countries of China and the USSR were enemies. China feared that the USSR would attack, so it built a huge network of escape tunnels and shelters beneath Beijing. Now some are part of the underground transport system, while others are shops, restaurants, and even skating rinks.

Gift stalls clutter popular ▲ tourist sections of the Great Wall. But they cannot disguise the structure's vast size or block the impressive views from the top.

OPEN SPACES

As the sun rises in Beijing, many people make their way to the city's parks and gardens. Some practice their *tai chi* and *qigong* exercises in the early morning light. Others play Chinese chess or Chinese music. Some even take their larks and other chirruping caged birds for a walk. Before the working day has begun, the capital's green spaces are humming with activity.

Beihai Park

Beihai (North Lake) Park lies northwest of the Forbidden City. The lake after which the park is named was probably dug in the 12th century. The rubble removed was later used to build Jade Island in the middle. On the island is the 115-foot-high (35m-high) White Dagoba (a place of worship), which was built almost 350 years ago. Beihai Park is especially popular in winter, when the lake ices over and skaters glide across it.

The White Dagoba in Beihai Park ▲ was built in honor of the Dalai Lama, a Tibetan Buddhist leader.

THE MING TOMBS

Thirteen of China's sixteen Ming emperors are buried in a valley about 30 miles (48 km) northwest of central Beijing. To reach it, people travel along a 4-mile (7-km) "spirit way." Huge stone statues of officials and animals (left) stand on either side of the route. Changling, the final resting place of Emperor Yongle (see page 9), is the largest tomb on the site and one of several open to the public. Many visitors have picnics in the valley. Some also enjoy its newer attractions, such as the Nine Dragons Amusement Park.

The Summer Palaces

Two famous parks lie in the far northwest of Beijing. The Old Summer Palace was where the emperors spent their summers until its buildings and gardens were almost completely destroyed in the Second Opium War (see page 9). Now people can wander among the ruins. The new Summer Palace is a huge park that covers about 800 acres (323 hectares) and is mostly covered by Kunming Lake. The park contains more than 100 buildings.

Jingshan Park

Beijing's Jingshan Park contains the famous Jingshan (Prospect Hill), which is made of mud dug up when the moat around the Forbidden City was made. The hill stands north of the city to block evil forces, which the ancient Chinese believed came from the north (see page 19). Many people climb Jingshan to admire the view across Beijing. Some visit its eastern slope to see the place where the last Ming emperor hanged himself in 1644.

Empress Cixi ordered the ▲ construction of this two-tier Marble Boat pavilion. It stands on the edge of Kunming Lake.

Beijing Zoo

Beijing Zoo began as a private park for Empress Cixi (see page 9). At first it contained only about 700 animals, but now has thousands. These include four giant pandas from the bamboo forests of southwest China. The zoo's gardens and lakes are well kept, but the animals live in cramped cages and are often treated badly by visitors.

◄ Colorful plaster statues peer out from the plants in Jingshan Park. Sometimes actors recreate an imperial procession in the park, complete with music and dancing.

HOMES AND HOUSING

For hundreds of years most Beijing citizens, from workers to nobles, lived in single-story houses grouped around courtyards. These lined the old, narrow lanes of the city, called hutongs. Since the **Communists** came to power, many people have moved into high-rise tower blocks.

◄ A woman washes the dishes in the tranquil courtyard of her house. Many homes like these line Beijing's hutongs.

In July 1976 a devastating ▼ earthquake hit northeast China. Many survivors went to Beijing, where they had to live in temporary shelters.

Hutongs

Beijing's hutongs grew up during the years of the Mongol Yuan dynasty (see page 8). One theory about why these lanes formed is that Chinese people built walls between their houses to keep out the Mongols, who often rode past. These walls joined to form many narrow walkways.

Lane names

People who shared an occupation often lived in the same hutong, which was then named after them. For example, the inhabitants of Clothes-Washing Hutong cleaned the emperors' clothes. Other hutongs were named after the large families who lived there, or according to their shape. Trousers Hutong begins as a single lane, then divides into two "legs."

Courtyard houses

Beijing's courtyard houses are hidden behind the hutong walls. To enter, people walk through a wooden doorway and around a **ghost wall**. Some houses have just one courtyard. Others have several courtyards and sometimes two "ear courtyards" at the sides as well. Most of these large houses once belonged to a single rich family. After the Communist takeover, the houses were subdivided to provide homes for three or more families.

FENG SHUI

Many of Beijing's old houses were built according to the 7,000-year-old theories of feng shui. This "science of winds and waters" teaches that negative yin forces and positive yang forces flow through the world. It is important to place buildings in a way that blocks yin and captures yang. As the south is believed to be the source of yang forces, imperial palaces and many courtyard houses face in that direction.

New homes

In 1953 the Communist government began the construction of many new housing estates on the outskirts of Beijing. Apartment blocks were later built in the city center as well. These modern homes are popular because, unlike courtyard houses, they have running water, electricity, and gas. About three-quarters of the city's population lives in them.

Satellite towns

The Beijing authorities are trying to prevent the population of the city's 10 crowded central districts from growing any larger. To do this they have built **satellite towns** of concrete tower blocks in the rural counties nearby. They have also helped industries set up factories and offices there to provide local jobs.

Pictures like this ▶ often hang in the kitchens of courtyard houses. They show "kitchen gods," who are said to bless food and protect cooks.

EDUCATION

When the **Communists** came to power in 1949, 80 percent of the population of China could not read or write. The government set out to provide education for everyone. By 2010, 94 percent of the population over age 15 was literate, and four of every five persons completed a secondary education.

University students ▲ hold up copies of *The Little Red Book* by Mao Zedong. Everyone studied this book during the Cultural Revolution.

Communist schools

After 1949 the Communists opened thousands of nurseries. Most of these were attached to factories or other workplaces, so that mothers could work while their children were cared for nearby. Large numbers of primary and secondary schools were also set up across China. The Communists hoped to give country peasants the same chances to learn as people in cities.

Two happy young children eat their lunch ▲ at a factory-based nursery in Beijing.

The Cultural Revolution

In 1966 Mao began the **Cultural Revolution** to protect his strict policies from reformers. Millions of pupils became Red Guards (members of a Communist youth movement), and schools were closed. They reopened in 1967, and pupils spent almost all their time studying Mao's writings and having military training. Some Red Guards beat and even killed teachers. In 1968 the army restored calm. Pupils were then sent to the country to learn "revolutionary values" from peasants.

Schools today

Mao's eventual successor, Deng Xiaoping, restored the old school system. Children in Beijing and other cities now receive a government-paid, nine-year primary and junior secondary school (middle school) education beginning at age six. There, they learn to read and write the complex Chinese language. It contains more than 50,000 **characters**, but most people use only about 8,000. At age 15, many pupils then carry on for three extra years if they choose. Others attend schools that train them for particular careers.

IMPERIAL EXAMS

In 165 BC Emperor Wendi introduced an examination for people who wanted to join the **civil service**. It tested their knowledge of Confucius (see page 22). By the time of the Ming dynasty, civil service exams were more complicated and scholars prepared for them at Beijing's Imperial College (above). Then they sat in cubicles for three days, scribbling down all they knew. The names of those who passed were carved on stone tablets in the city's Confucius Temple. The exams were abolished in 1905.

▲ Today, university students enjoy all the benefits of higher education, including the latest in computer equipment.

Higher education

China's universities and colleges were closed at the beginning of the Cultural Revolution, then began to reopen in 1970. Today Beijing contains about 50 places of higher education, many in the northwestern Haidian District. These include Beijing University, which was founded in 1898. The nearby Qinghua University and Chinese Academy of Sciences are among the most famous centers of scientific education and research in China.

RELIGION

 Before **Communist** days, most people in Beijing followed the philosophies of **Daoism, Confucianism,** and **Buddhism**, often combining all three. The Communists tried to stop these practices, and many places of worship were closed or destroyed during the Cultural Revolution. After Mao's death, religious persecution officially ended, and in 1982 everyone was granted freedom of belief. But the government is still suspicious of organized religion.

Daoist monks had to ▲ work as farm laborers during the Cultural Revolution. Many have now returned to their temples, where they are free to study and pray.

Daoism

Daoism developed in China in the 6th century BC, but Beijing's oldest Daoist temple, the Temple of the White Cloud, dates back only to the Tang dynasty (618–907 BCE). The temple's oldest shrine, or place of worship, contains statues of 60 gods. Each god rules over one of the 60 years in the Chinese calendar. Visitors come to the shrine and pray to the god of the year in which they were born.

Confucianism

Confucius was a wise man who traveled around China in the 5th century BC. He taught that people could create a good society if they acted with respect, obedience, and compassion. Confucianism became the basis of imperial government, and ceremonies to honor Confucius and his ancestors took place in Beijing's Confucius Temple.

This painting shows an imaginary ➤ meeting between Confucius (far right) and Lao Zi, the traditional founder of Daoism.

 A woman prays at a shrine in Beijing's Lama Temple. The monks who live in the temple usually pray privately early in the day.

Buddhism

Buddhism arrived in China from India in about the 1st century AD. The most famous Buddhist temple in central Beijing is the Lama Temple. It was built in 1694 as a palace, but was later turned into a monastery for Tibetan Buddhist monks. The temple was not damaged in the Cultural Revolution, and Yellow Hat monks now carry out regular rituals there. It has five main halls, as well as the Wanfu Pavilion, which contains a 60-foot-high (18m-high) statue of the Buddha.

CHRISTIANITY IN CHINA

During the 16th century, Roman Catholic **Jesuit** priests came to China to spread Christian ideas. The main Catholic church in modern Beijing is South Cathedral. It is run by an association of Chinese Catholics, as the Roman Catholic Church is banned in China. Protestant churches in Beijing include the Rice Market Church, built in the 1920s.

Non-Muslims may go into the ▼ courtyard of the splendid Niujie Mosque, but they are not allowed to enter the main prayer hall.

Beijing's Muslims

Beijing has a large minority population of Muslims (see page 13). They worship in dozens of mosques across the city. The two most popular: the 10th-century Niujie Mosque, which is the largest and oldest in the capital; and the 15th-century Dongsi Mosque. The Niujie Mosque, which originally was built in 996, has a large prayer hall and the Tower for Observing the Moon. Muslims watch the moon there every year to work out when the period of **Ramadan** starts and ends.

INDUSTRY AND AGRICULTURE

 Industry in Beijing has grown under **Communist** rule, along with agriculture. The eight rural counties that surround Beijing (see page 5) produce much of the city's food.

 Automobile manufacturing is among the many industries that have thrived in the Beijing area.

Communist plans

From 1953 Mao Zedong's government introduced a series of **Five-Year Plans** to encourage industrial growth in China. Private businesses were taken over by the state, and foreign investment was banned. Factories were built in many areas, including Beijing, where there had not been much industry before. But major problems followed. In 1958 the government put into action a plan called the **Great Leap Forward**. The idea was to make everyone work hard to expand agriculture and industry as fast as possible. The plan was a disaster, and in fact made the country's economy even worse. Mao's government also refused to let China trade with other countries, which held it back.

MONEY MATTERS

The People's Bank of China is based in Beijing. It is the bank of the Chinese government and issues Chinese currency. It is also in charge of the Bank of China, which deals with the growing amount of foreign trade. In 1995 foreign banks opened in Beijing for the first time. Most of Beijing's financial dealings take place in a 40-block area called Beijing Financial Street (left), sometimes known as "China's Wall Street."

Major World Cities

Modern industry

In the late 1970s, Deng Xiaoping (see page 21) set out to modernize Chinese industry and agriculture, and to improve the economy. Private businesses were allowed again, and foreign investment and technology were welcomed. More and more goods were produced and, despite the disturbances of 1989 (see page 11), government and foreign money poured into Beijing.

Small arts and crafts industries still flourish ▲ in Beijing, for example painting on silk (above), enamel-making, and embroidery.

The cost of change

These reforms have given ordinary Chinese people many new opportunities, for example the chance to set up in business. People have had more leisure time since the working week was reduced from six days to five in 1995. There are drawbacks to the changes, too. Although millions still work for state-owned companies, there is no longer guaranteed employment and food. There are growing numbers of jobless young people in Beijing.

Main industries

Beijing has many successful industries, dominated by services such as finance, real estate, and information technology. Manufacuring and construction also still accounts for about one-fifth of the economic output. However, several high-polluting, high-energy-consuming business have been relocated outside of the city in recent years.

Farming in Beijing

The municipality of Beijing has eight rural counties. The farmers from these areas supply fruits, nuts, wood, vegetables, wheat, and other products to the city areas of Beijing.

◄ Northern China is not ideal for farming, as the weather can be cold and there are often droughts. Yet vegetable crops thrive in irrigation channels (left) in the countryside around Beijing.

CRIME AND PUNISHMENT

During the imperial era, serious criminals were judged and punished by the emperors. Verdicts were announced from the Forbidden City's Wumen (Meridian Gate), and disobedient officials were publicly whipped there. After 1949 China's **Communist** government introduced a new justice system. Now law and order in Beijing is upheld by the Public Security Bureau (police), procurators, and the People's Courts.

Beijing police

Public Security Bureau (police) members are a common sight in Beijing. They wear white hats and uniforms with a red trim and often travel on foot or on motorbikes. The police usually have the right to decide if a suspect is guilty and to choose a punishment. This may be a fine, time in prison or a labor camp, or even execution.

◄ This 19th-century painting shows a Chinese prisoner in chains. He is waiting to be judged and sentenced.

Street wardens

Beijing is divided into many small areas, each with its own street committee run by local Communist Party members. The committees organize groups of volunteer wardens, who patrol the streets and combat crimes from rubbish-dumping to burglary. The wardens, most of them women, are easy to recognize because they wear red armbands marked with the words "On Duty." The wardens also help the community by caring for the sick, the old, and the unemployed. They check on pregnancies in each family and monitor family activities.

City crimes

Theft is one of the most common crimes in Beijing. Pickpockets operate in the streets and on the city's crowded transport networks, often using razors to cut bags open. Thieves also regularly steal bicycles from their streetside parking places. A major crime in Beijing is piracy (illegal copying) of computer software, CDs, DVDs, and books. Antique smuggling is also common. Serious violent crimes such as assault and murder are rare.

The court system

The police do not always have the right to judge and punish offenders. The most serious crimes are referred to procurators, whose job is to decide if people should go on trial. Trials take place in front of judges at People's Courts. They are often held in private, and there is never a jury. The most important court in China is the Supreme People's Court in Beijing, where crimes against the state are tried.

After the death of Mao Zedong in 1976, his wife, Jiang Qing (above), and three others tried to seize power. The "Gang of Four" was arrested, and Jiang Qing was sentenced to death at a Beijing court. It was later changed to life imprisonment. ▲

◄ The main job of the Beijing police is to catch criminals, but they also keep the busy traffic in the city under control.

CHOP CHEATING

Most Chinese adults have one or more chops. These are small blocks carved with the characters of the owner's name. People dip the chops in red ink, then use them as seals to "sign" official documents (left). There is a thriving trade in stolen and fake chops, just as there is in stolen credit cards in other countries.

GETTING AROUND

Beijing is the center of China's rail, road, and air networks. Since the **Communist** takeover in 1949, all its transport systems have been expanded and improved. It's been necessary to cope with ever-growing increases in traffic and population.

Every day, commuters ▲ stream onto and out of train cars on Beijing's sleek, high-speed rail system.

Rail travel

The railway is China's most widely used means of transport. High-speed lines link Beijing to many other Chinese cities, including Harbin, Shanghai, Guangzhou, and Jiulong in Hong Kong (see page 43). The Trans-Siberian Railway runs from Beijing to Moscow in Russia. Direct routes also go to Mongolia, North Korea, and Vietnam. "Soft-seat" class is more comfortable—and more expensive—than "hard-seat" class.

The Beijing underground

For a long time, the Beijing subway system operated with only two lines. In recent years, though, the underground has expanded to eight lines in the inner city and eight more to the outer districts. Even more new lines are in the works. It is a quick, modern, and safe way to get around.

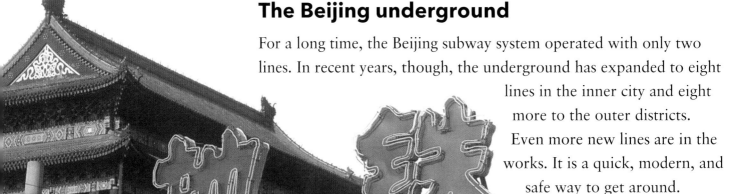

◄ A Beijing underground sign. Underground trains run every few minutes at busy times. Cost is based on distance traveled.

Bicycles and cars

Beijing was once a dream city for cyclists, as they could make fast progress across its flat ground. But as China grows richer, car ownership is increasing. As a result, cycling is becoming more dangerous—and all cyclists have to breathe exhaust-polluted air. Builders are now constructing new roads for all the extra traffic. There are six ring roads around the city center, and a seventh is scheduled to open in 2017. These roads are becoming just as busy as Chang'an Boulevard, the main route across Beijing.

Bicyclists compete with buses, taxis, and ▲ other cars on the busy roads in Beijing.

THE GRAND CANAL

The emperors of the Sui dynasty (581–618 AD) built the Grand Canal (above) to link the rice-producing regions of the south with cities further to the north. Khubilai Khan extended the canal to his capital Dadu (see page 8). The Ming emperor Yongle used the canal to bring not only food but also building materials for the Forbidden City to Beijing. Today the Grand Canal is China's busiest inland waterway.

Beijing buses

Buses, minibuses, and trolley buses all make their way around Beijing. Although bus travel is cheap, it is often far from pleasant. People have to push and shove their way on, then endure slow rides in overcrowded vehicles. Announcements in English have made it a bit better recently for non-Chinese-speaking riders.

Air travel

Beijing's Capital International Airport is about 17 miles (27 km) northeast of the city center. Flights depart from there to more than 600 towns and cities within the country, as well as to overseas destinations. Three terminals serve passengers in the world's second-busiest airport.

SHOPS AND MARKETS

 Modern, multi-story shopping centers have arrived in Beijing, but there are still many traditional shops and markets to explore. Shoppers have to be on their guard against poor-quality goods and fake antiques. They also have to bargain hard in markets if they want good prices.

Shopping paradise

Wangfujing, to the east of the Forbidden City, is the biggest and most fashionable shopping street in Beijing. Old, low-level shops nestle among the growing number of large, high-rise stores. The largest of them all is the Beijing Department Store, but the stores in the new Xindong'an Shopping Center, which opened in 1998, are far more luxurious.

◄ Shoppers flock to the stores on Wangfujing, even at night.

MYSTERIOUS MEDICINES

Whenever the emperors of the Qing dynasty were feeling unwell, they had medicines prepared for them at Tongrentang Pharmacy in Dazhalan Hutong. The shop has existed since 1669, and the doctors who now work there still make many of the old potions, using the same ingredients. These include sea horses, snake wine, and stag antlers, as well as a huge variety of herbs. Today anyone can visit the pharmacy in search of a cure.

Qianmen and Dazhalan

Qianmen (Front Gate), south of Tiananmen Square, once marked the boundary between the tranquil Inner City and the bustling Outer City, which was full of shops, theaters, and teahouses. Qianmen Street runs south from the gate. Stores there sell everything from silk to musical instruments. Dazhalan Hutong, off Qianmen Street, has many silk shops and Beijing's oldest delicatessen. There is also a famous pharmacy (see left).

◄ The interior of a shopping mall in Beijing. It includes many of the same stores found in any Western city.

Friendship Store

The Jianguomenwai area of east Beijing houses many foreign embassies, so luxurious shops have grown up nearby to cater to their staff. The most famous is the Friendship Store. Once only foreigners and **Communist** Party officials were allowed in, but now anyone can go in. It stocks Chinese arts and crafts, groceries, and books.

Art and antiques

Liulichang Street (Glazed Tile Street), southwest of the Forbidden City, was where the yellow roof tiles of the imperial palaces were made. In recent years the street has been restored so that it looks as it did during the Qing dynasty. Shops in Liulichang specialize in paintings, books, and **calligraphy** materials such as brushes, paper, and ink. Many also sell antiques, but they are often not genuine.

Market day

Every Sunday a special market is held in Panjiayuan, in Beijing's eastern suburbs. Here ordinary people, especially farmers from the country around Beijing, sell goods from their own homes. Bargain hunters may find a real antique or a beautiful, handwoven carpet. Even if they aren't lucky, it's fun just to look around.

Longtan Park in ➤ southeast Beijing hosts a regular bird market. Here, a group of men gather to chat before buying and selling their birds.

FOOD AND DRINK

Chinese food is famous all over the world. The country has four main regional styles of cooking: Cantonese, Sichuanese, Eastern, and Northern. All can be sampled in Beijing restaurants, but at home, people eat their own Northern cuisine.

Home cooking

Family meals in Beijing consist of many dishes. First there may be a selection of cold starters, including pickled vegetables. Then hot meat, fish, and vegetable dishes are served—for example, chicken flavored with garlic and ginger. These are often eaten with noodles or dumplings, made from wheat grown locally, rather than rice, which comes from the south. People scoop food from the serving dishes into their bowls, then eat using chopsticks. Meals usually end with clear soup and jasmine tea.

An impressive feast ▲ covers this table in a Chinese family home. The dishes are placed in the middle so that everyone can share.

▲ The Mongol**s** once cooked meat in their battle helmets, but now Mongolian hotpot is prepared in dishes used only for cooking.

Beijing restaurants

Mao Zedong did not approve of restaurants, so while he was in power most Beijing eating places closed down. Many have opened since then, serving both Chinese and foreign food. Several restaurants specialize in Beijing Duck, a dish created for the emperors. It consists of duck coated with vinegar, honey, and water, then dried, grilled, and served with pancakes and **hoisin sauce**. Another Beijing speciality is Mongolian hotpot: strips of vegetables and lamb that diners cook in a pot at their table.

Chinese fast food is ➤ not always finger food. Diners at this streetside kiosk in Beijing pick up each mouthful with chopsticks.

Imperial cuisine

China's emperors invited top chefs from all over the country to work in the palace kitchens, where they prepared vast banquets. Empress Cixi (see page 9) demanded meals of 128 dishes every day. As she never ate them all, the chefs served the old dishes over and over again, and were only found out when maggots started to crawl across the table. Some expensive Beijing restaurants now serve imperial cuisine. Among the most famous is Fangshan, in Beihai Park.

Fast food

All sorts of fast food are available from Beijing street stalls. Steamed bread, dumplings, and spring rolls—for example, made with prawns or vegetables—are popular all year round. In winter many people eat baked sweet potatoes, cooked in ovens made from oil drums. Western fast food outlets also attract large crowds, particularly young people. There are hamburger, pizza, and fried-chicken restaurants all over the city.

TIME FOR TEA

Soft drinks are popular in modern Beijing. Many Chinese men in the capital also drink beer and grain spirits, such as the famous Maotai. Almost everyone's favorite drink is tea (left), which has been common in China since the Tang dynasty (618–907). Chinese people drink both black tea and green tea, always without milk. One favorite is oolong, a strong, dark brew whose name means "black dragon." Tea is enjoyed either at home or in one of the city's teahouses, along with snacks such as dried fruit.

ENTERTAINMENT

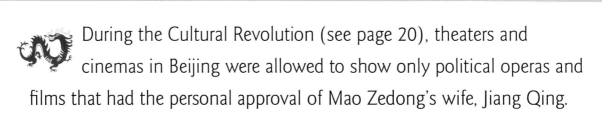

During the Cultural Revolution (see page 20), theaters and cinemas in Beijing were allowed to show only political operas and films that had the personal approval of Mao Zedong's wife, Jiang Qing. Since Mao's death, the city's entertainment scene has come back to life.

An actor dressed for ▲ a *dan* (female) role in a Beijing opera. Men played all the female parts in the past, but now women sing and act, too.

Beijing Opera

Beijing Opera developed in the late 18th century. The operas told stories of love, war, loyalty, and betrayal. Their mixture of singing, speech, mime, dance, and acrobatics became popular with ordinary people as well as emperors. The actors' elaborate costumes and makeup added to the attraction. People can still see opera in Beijing. Traditional shows are six-hour events. Others have the performance time cut to two hours.

Beijing theater

There was no speech-only theater in China until the early years of the 20th century. Now plays are performed at several Beijing venues, including the Beijing Exhibition Center Theater. At first, most productions in the city were Chinese versions of plays by foreign writers such as William Shakespeare. Today the works of a bold new generation of Chinese dramatists often appear.

Cinema culture

Filmgoing is popular in China and, since the 1980s, filmmaking also has increased. In Beijing, as elsewhere in the country, most people prefer action-packed, martial-arts epics. Some Beijing cinemas show foreign films, but they are all checked by the **Communist** government. Only a few dozen are allowed into China each year.

Amazing acrobatics

The spectacular routines of China's acrobats developed from everyday activities such as climbing up bamboo poles. The first state-run group of acrobats, the China Acrobatic Troupe, was founded in 1950. It gives regular, breath-taking performances at Beijing's Universal Theater. Other groups display their skills at Chaoyang Theater and at Beijing Amusement Park, where there are also many rides to enjoy.

Making music

Performances of both Chinese and Western classical music take place at the Beijing Concert Hall. Many of the capital's residents now prefer to listen to pop music. The British band Wham! and the American singer John Denver were among the first to bring pop to Beijing. Nowadays the city's growing number of discos play tracks by many foreign artists, as well as Chinese stars. Beijing's young people often spend evenings there or at one of the city's lively karaoke bars.

Chinese acrobats ➤ begin their training as young children. It takes years of practice to become as skillful as this.

PUPPET PLAY

Traditional Chinese puppeteers perform fascinating shows at several Beijing venues (left). At the China Puppet Theater in Chaoyang District, plays are performed using both glove and shadow puppets. Puppetry is often a part of variety shows that also include magic, juggling, singing, and comedy routines. Puppet shows are popular with children and adults, but skilled puppeteers are becoming rare.

MUSEUMS AND GALLERIES

Many of Beijing's antiques and works of art have been lost or destroyed in recent years. In 1949 the Nationalists were defeated by the **Communists** (see page 11) and took many priceless objects to Taiwan. Many more treasures were destroyed in the Cultural Revolution. The Chinese government is now collecting as many lost pieces of art as possible, and will display them in the capital's museums.

Millions of years ago, ➤ dinosaurs roamed China. Now visitors can see some of their giant skeletons in Beijing's Natural History Museum.

The Palace Museum

There are more than 50 museums in Beijing. The most magnificent of all is the Palace Museum, the official name of the Forbidden City. As well as the main halls and palaces, it contains buildings such as the Hall of Jewellery, where visitors can admire a gold pagoda, and the Hall of Clocks, where exquisite timepieces from both China and Europe chime away the hours.

The Natural History Museum

Thousands of plant and animal species, as well as an exhibition on human evolution, are displayed in the four halls of Beijing's Natural History Museum. Some of the most prized exhibits are fossilized dinosaur bones. These include the spectacular, long-necked skeleton of a creature called a Mamenchisaurus, which was found in Sichuan, China.

THE ANCIENT OBSERVATORY

The Chinese emperors wanted to please Heaven (see page 15), so their officials "read" the skies to see if they had done so. They also made measurements of star and planet movements to create an accurate calendar. The Ming emperors built an observatory in Beijing and employed Jesuit priests as astronomers. Fifteen bronze instruments were used in the observatory. Today, eight of these fascinating instruments remain. Visitors can climb to the roof of the observatory (right) to see them.

The Museum of Chinese History

A four-story building in Tiananmen Square houses two of Beijing's most important museums: the Museum of Chinese History and the Museum of the Revolution. The Museum of Chinese History contains more than 30,000 objects that tell China's story from the earliest times until 1919. They include **oracle bones,** porcelain vases, and silk embroideries. The museum also has exhibitions such as Chinese inventions, including printing.

The Museum of the Revolution

The Museum of the Revolution continues the story of China's history from 1919, when Communist ideas began to take hold in the country (see page 10). The museum covers the founding of the Communist Party, the civil war between Communists and Nationalists, and the struggle against the Japanese. Finally, documents and photographs illustrate the Communist victory of 1949.

The China Art Gallery

The China Art Gallery, near Jingshan Park, was built in 1959. Delicate ink paintings by traditional Chinese artists are displayed in its huge exhibition areas, alongside works by some of the country's more adventurous modern painters. Sometimes traveling exhibitions of foreign works are on view.

◄ This bronze wine jug dates from the time of the Zhou dynasty (1027–771 BCE). The Museum of Chinese History contains many fascinating artifacts like this.

The people of Beijing celebrate two types of festivals: traditional festivals that began in pre-Communist times, and new festivals that have developed since the Communist takeover.

◀ Chinese New Year banners decorate the entrance to this house. They are designed to bring good luck in the coming months.

New Year

The first day of January is an official holiday in China. But Chinese New Year, known as the Spring Festival, is much more important. Chinese New Year's Day falls between January 21 and February 20, when the year's first new moon appears. The night before, families clean their houses, eat a special meal, and let off firecrackers at midnight. Over the next few days, lion dances and other colorful celebrations continue in the streets.

The Lantern Festival

The Spring Festival ends when the first full moon of the New Year arrives. On that night, the Lantern Festival takes place. People make colorful lanterns from silk and paper, hang some outside their homes, and carry others in processions through the streets. Lantern candles often caused fires in the past. Many original Forbidden City buildings burned down in Lantern Festival blazes and had to be replaced.

A huge crowd watches fireworks exploding ▶ in the night sky during Beijing's National Day festivities. It is a spectacular sight.

Performers celebrate ➤
International Labor Day with a
traditional waist-drum dance.

May Holidays

The first big Communist festival
of the year takes place on May 1,
International Labor Day. This is an
official holiday, so almost everyone
in Beijing is free to wander the city
and celebrate the achievements of
Communism around the world. The
capital is decorated with flowers
to add to the festive atmosphere.
Three days later, National Youth
Day takes place. This unofficial
holiday honors the protests of May
4, 1919 (see page 10).

Autumn double

Two major events take place in the autumn. The
traditional Mid-Autumn (Moon) Festival is celebrated
in September or October. It is a time when Beijing
citizens simply admire the moon's beauty. They also
eat sweet **moon cakes.** On October 1, National Day,
the city remembers the birth of the People's Republic
of China (see page 11). Crowds fill the streets to see
spectacular floral displays and military parades.

QING MING

Qing Ming is an ancient festival that takes place on April 5. On
this day in the past, Chinese people cleaned their relatives' graves,
then laid flowers and burnt **ghost money** there. These rituals are
now less common in Beijing, but people still remember dead family
members at this time. Some people also lay wreaths in Tiananmen
Square to honor soldiers who died fighting for Communism.

CITY CHARACTERS

China's emperors had supreme power in Beijing until 1911 and controlled the life of the capital. Yet people of other ranks and nationalities have played a major part in shaping the city, both before and since the emperors.

Chabi

The success of Khubilai Khan's reign in Dadu (see page 8) owed much to Chabi, his favorite wife. Chabi's aim was to make her husband's Yuan dynasty great, so she helped him make policies that were suited to Chinese people. For example, she persuaded Khubilai to support farming, even though this was unfamiliar to the Mongols. She also designed a uniform with a brimmed hat and sleeveless top for his armies to wear in China's hot regions.

Emperor Qianlong

The Qing emperor Qianlong ruled from 1736 to 1795. During his reign, China's armies conquered vast areas of land. Qianlong was a scholar as well as a military leader. He studied in the Forbidden City's Hall of Mental Cultivation and had all the books in China arranged into the 36,000 volumes of the *Four Treasuries*. He also added European-style buildings to the Old Summer Palace (see page 17). But Qianlong's reign ended badly, as population growth led to food shortages and riots. He died in 1799.

▼ In this beautiful 18th-century scroll, men from the region of Kirghiz in central Siberia present a horse to Emperor Qianlong as tribute.

▲ Song Qingling with her husband Sun Yat-sen in 1921. Her sister married Chiang Kai-shek, Sun's successor as leader of the Nationalists (see page 11).

MARCO POLO

Marco Polo (above, in pink) was a Venetian who probably set out for China in 1271, when he was just 17. He arrived in Dadu more than three years later, and was amazed by its splendor. The Yuan ruler Khubilai Khan gave Marco a job that involved traveling around the Mongol Empire. The young man kept records of his journeys, which were published some years after his return to Europe in 1295. The tales astonished the Western world.

Song Qingling

Song Qingling was the wife of the Nationalist leader Sun Yat-sen (see page 10). She supported the Nationalist cause for many years, but in 1949 she sided with the Communists. Later she worked for the poor and founded the China Welfare Institute. From 1963 until her death in 1981, Song Qingling lived in a house in northwest Beijing. Now it is a museum devoted to her life.

This photograph ➤ of Xu Wenli was taken in his home in early 1994.

Xu Wenli

China's democracy movement began to grow in the late 1970s. At that time Xu Wenli, a Beijing electrician, was editor of a pro-democracy magazine called *April Fifth Forum*. Xu, who later became the leader of the illegal China Democratic Party, twice was arrested by the Chinese government for his political activities, and spent 16 years in prison. He was exiled to the United States in 2002.

BEIJING'S FUTURE

  Beijing has changed a lot in the last several decades. Building work has transformed its appearance. Wealth has increased, but so has pollution and traffic. The city is more open to the Western world and has adopted some of its ways—but not its democracy.

Building boom

Builders are still hard at work in Beijing, tearing down old walls, streets, and houses. China has undergone such dramatic change over the past few decades that it has been called a "Second Industrial Revolution." But the city government also realizes that parts of old Beijing are worth keeping. So demolition may slow down, but it will not stop.

▼ The Italian opera *Turandot* is set in China. Europeans were not welcome in China during the Mao years, so it could not be performed there. In 1998 the opera was staged in the Forbidden City. Members of the Chinese army played the drums.

Tourist trade

There were no real tourists in Beijing before the late 1970s. Almost all foreign visitors were politicians, business people, or journalists. Now the tourist trade is booming: The city hosts more than 4 million international visitors each year. Beijing provides hotels and other facilities for visitors. New plans for the city include restoring many top tourist destinations.

Looking at law

The Chinese government is shaping a new legal system for the country. It has passed more than 300 new laws on this subject since the 1980s. All law firms used to be run by the state, but now some private firms have opened in Beijing. Western governments and human rights organizations still want China to make its system more open—for example, by having jury trials and allowing public court hearings.

Beijing business

China is one of the world's largest producers of goods and services, and its largest exporter. The country's economy grew at a robust rate for much of the 2000s before posting its slowest growth in a quarter of a century in 2015. That unsettled investors around the world. Still, many foreign companies, from fast food chains to car manufacturers, have a base in Beijing.

Political uncertainty

On July 1 1997, the former British **colony** of Hong Kong, which was a democracy, returned to Chinese Communist rule. Many Hong Kong people were unhappy about that. In early 1998, a period known as the "Beijing Spring," the Chinese government seemed to be growing more tolerant of democratic ideas. But in December, many rebels such as Xu Wenli (see page 41) were arrested as the goverment returned to cracking down on top dissidents. In 2011, highly visible artist and political activist Ai Weiwei was arrested, possibly to set an example that no one is immune from government reach.

Olympic Games

At the Summer Olympic Games in 2008, Beijing hosted more than 10,000 athletes who competed in 302 events. Although there was some controversy—thousands of residents in the city's hutongs (see page 18) were displaced by construction—the Games generally were considered a success. Now, Beijing is slated to host the Winter Olympics in 2022. It will become the first city ever to host both a Summer Games and a Winter Games.

▲ Beijing National Stadium, which was built for the Summer Olympic Games in 2008, hosted the World Championships in track and field in 2015 (above).

TIMELINE

This timeline shows some of the most important dates in Beijing's history. All the events are mentioned earlier in this book.

6TH CENTURY BCE

Daoism develops in China

c 5TH CENTURY

First city grows up on the site of Beijing
Confucianism develops in China

3RD CENTURY

First city destroyed and new city built
Northern defensive walls linked to form the first Great Wall of China

1ST CENTURY

165
Emperor Wendi introduces an examination for people who want to join the civil service

1ST CENTURY CE

Buddhism arrives in China from India

10TH CENTURY

The Khitan invade northern China and take over the city. They make it their second capital and call it Yanjing.

Some Chinese people convert to Islam and become the Hui minority

12TH CENTURY

The Jurchen defeat the Khitan and rename their city Zhongdu

13TH CENTURY

1215
Zhongdu is burned to the ground by the Mongols, led by Genghis Khan
1266
Khubilai Khan builds a new city north of Zhongdu. It becomes the capital of the Mongol Empire.
1279-1368
Rule of the Mongol Yuan dynasty

14TH CENTURY

1368
Chinese rebels drive out the Mongols and set up the Ming dynasty

15TH CENTURY

1403
Emperor Yongle comes to power
1406
Construction work begins on a new city, including the Forbidden City, south of the Mongol capital
1421
Forbidden City is completed
Yongle moves in to his new capital and calls it Beijing, meaning "Northern Capital"

16TH CENTURY

Jesuit monks arrive in China and begin
to preach Christianity

17TH CENTURY

1644

Manchus invade China, defeat the Ming and
establish the Qing dynasty

18TH CENTURY

1736-1795

Rule of Emperor Qianlong

19TH CENTURY

1839-1842

First Opium War between China and Britain

1850-1864

Taiping Rebellion takes place

1856-1860

Second Opium War between China and Britain

1895

Japan defeats China

20TH CENTURY

1900

Boxer Rebellion takes place

1911

Revolts against imperial rule break out
across China

1912

Republican government led by Sun Yat-sen
established but fails to hold power

1914-1918

World War I takes place

1919

Protests in Beijing against foreign interference

1921

Chinese Communist Party founded

1923

Kuomintang government set up in Guangzhou

1925

Sun Yat-sen dies; Chiang Kai-shek takes
over leadership of Kuomintang

1928

Kuomintang seizes power and sets up
a government in Nanjing

1937

Japanese troops occupy Beijing and remain
there until 1945

1945

Kuomintang return to power

1949

Communists led by Mao Zedong overthrow
the Kuomintang

People's Republic of China founded

1966

Cultural Revolution launched; schools
and universities close

1967

Schools reopen

1970s

One-child policy introduced

1976

Death of Mao Zedong

1989

Pro-democracy demonstration in
Tiananmen Square crushed by the
People's Liberation Army

1995

Foreign banks open in Beijing for the first time

1997

Hong Kong returns to Chinese rule

21ST CENTURY

2008

Beijing hosts the Summer Olympic Games

2011

Artist and political activist Ai Weiwei is arrested

2016

China's long-standing one-child policy is
modified

GLOSSARY

Boxer   A member of a Chinese nationalist movement called The Society of Righteous and Harmonious Fists.

Buddhism   A philosophy that began in India in about 500 BC. It is based on the teaching of a prince called Gautama Siddhartha. He was later given the title "Buddha," which means "enlightened one."

calligraphy   Handwriting. In China, Japan, and many other countries, handwriting is regarded as an art.

character   A symbol used in writing. Chinese characters are not letters, as in English, but ideographs. This means that they represent ideas rather than sounds.

civil service   Staff who carry out government policies.

civil war   A war between different groups within a country rather than between separate countries.

colony   A land ruled by another country.

Communist (noun)   A person who believes in the principles of Communism (see below).

Communist (adjective)   Governed by or relating to the principles of Communism. This political and economic system aims to create a classless society. Communist countries are ruled by the unelected members of just one political party. Communist businesses are usually owned by the state rather than private individuals.

Confucianism   The teachings and practices of the moral system set up by the Chinese philosopher Confucius.

Cultural Revolution   A mass movement of the Chinese people that was begun by Mao Zedong in 1966. His aim was to get rid of old, non-Communist values and to punish people, such as intellectuals and artists, who opposed his ideas. The revolution began to fade in 1969, but did not officially end until Mao's death in 1976.

Daoism   A philosophy that developed in China in the 6th century BC. One branch of Daoism stresses the importance of living in harmony with the universe by following the *dao* (way). Another involves the worship of many gods.

democracy   A political system in which citizens elect the people who govern them.

Dowager Empress   The title given to a former empress once her husband, the emperor, has died.

dynasty   A family that rules a country for generations.

ethnic Chinese   Belonging to the Chinese race.

First World War   A major war that lasted from 1914 to 1918 and involved a large number of countries. Eventually, Germany and Austria-Hungary were defeated by Britain, Russia, France, and the United States.

Five-Year Plan   One of a series of plans for economic development in China. The first began in 1953.

Genghis Khan   The military and political leader who set up the Mongol Empire in 1206.

ghost money   Money burned at people's graves. According to ancient Chinese belief, the dead will then be able to use it in the afterlife.

ghost wall   A wall just inside the entrance of a house to keep ghosts out. The Chinese believe that ghosts travel only in straight lines, so cannot move around these walls to get inside houses.

Great Leap Forward   The plan to increase industrial and agricultural production in China that was launched in 1958. It was over ambitious and poorly organized, and ended in failure in 1960.

Greenwich Mean Time   The time in Greenwich, England, which stands on the zero line of longitude. It is used as a base for calculating the time in the rest of the world.

hoisin sauce   A dark, red-brown sauce made of soya beans, vinegar, sugar, and spices.

imperial   Relating to an empire, emperor, or empress.

Jesuit   A member of the Society of Jesus, an order of Roman Catholic priests that was founded in 1534.

Jurchen   A people from the region of Manchuria in northeast China. In 1115 they formed the Jin dynasty and ruled much of north China until the invasion of the Mongols.

Khitan   A people from the Liao Valley in Manchuria, northeast China. They set up the Liao Empire in 946, but in 1125 were defeated by the Jurchen and others.

Kuomintang   The Chinese National People's Party, which was founded in 1894. The Kuomintang fought the Communist Party for control of China for many years. After it was defeated, many of its members went to Taiwan, where the party still rules.

Manchu   A member of a people from Manchuria in northeast China who conquered the Chinese in 1644. The Manchus founded the imperial Qing dynasty.

Mongol   A member of a people from Mongolia that rose to power under the leadership of Genghis Khan.

moon cake   A cake in the shape of a full moon.

municipality   A city and surrounding district that has its own government.

nomad   A person who moves from place to place, searching, for example, for food or grazing land for animals.

Opium Wars   Two wars (the First Opium War, 1839–1842, and the Second Opium War, 1856–1860) between China and Britain. Britain wanted China to import the drug opium from British-ruled India in return for goods such as tea. The Chinese resisted but lost the wars. After the first war, China had to hand Hong Kong to Britain.

oracle bone   A tortoise or cattle bone that was heated in a fire until it cracked. People "read" the cracks to tell the future, and scratched the predictions on the bone.

qi gong   A martial art. By performing the breathing and other exercises of qigong, people hope to make their *qi* (life energy) flow through their bodies in the right way.

Ramadan   The ninth month of the Muslim year, when people fast during the hours of daylight.

republic   A country or other political unit with elected rulers and no emperor, king, or queen.

republican   Of or relating to a republic.

satellite town   A small town that grows up on the edge of a large town or city and depends on it for jobs.

Second World War   A major war that lasted from 1939 to 1945. Eventually, Britain, France, the USSR, and the United States defeated Germany, Italy, and Japan. During this war, Beijing was occupied by Japan.

symmetrical   Having exactly the same shape on either side of a central line. Beijing's Old City was built around an imaginary line running from north to south. Matching buildings and parks on either side of the line were designed to create balance.

tai chi   A martial art also known as shadow boxing. Its exercises are designed to encourage the correct flow of energy through the mind and body.

Taiping Rebellion   A major peasant rebellion against the Qing dynasty that began in 1850. Its leader was a Christian called Hong Xiuchuan. The rebellion ended in 1864 after about 20 million people had died.

INDEX